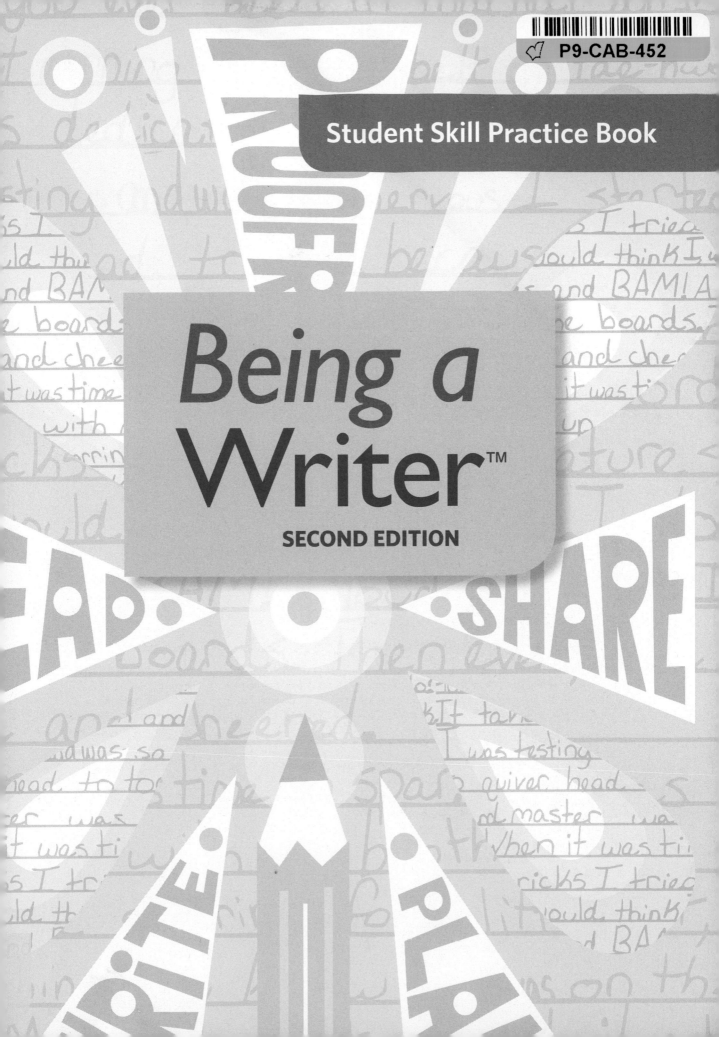

Student Skill Practice Book

Being a
Writer™

SECOND EDITION

Center for the Collaborative Classroom
1001 Marina Village Parkway, Suite 110
Alameda, CA 94501
(800) 666-7270; fax: (510) 464-3670
collaborativeclassroom.org

ISBN 978-1-61003-265-0

Printed in the United States of America

12 13 14 15 16 17 EBM 25 24 23 22 21 20 19 18

CONTENTS

(continues)

CONTENTS *(continued)*

Capitalization and Punctuation

Silly Sandwiches

A. Read each sentence. Underline the complete subject. Circle the simple subject.

1. (Lionel) loves all kinds of sandwiches.

2. His favorite (uncle) teaches him how to make unusual sandwiches.

3. One (sandwich) has pickles and peanut butter.

4. Lionel's older (sister) makes banana and peanut butter sandwiches.

5. The two (children) take pictures of their silly sandwiches.

× 5

B. Choose a simple subject from the word box to complete each sentence. Then circle the complete subject.

| neighbors | winner | rules | person | contest |

1. Some _neighbors_ are planning a sandwich-making contest.

2. The _contest_ takes place on Saturday.

3. The _rules_ are easy to follow.

4. Each _person_ makes one strange but tasty treat!

× 3

5. The _winner_ gets free sandwiches from the Yummy Sandwich Shop for one month.

C. Write a paragraph about your favorite sandwich. Use complete sentences.

Try It. You'll Like It!

A. Read each sentence. Underline the complete predicate. Write the simple predicate on the line.

1. Lola likes all kinds of food.

   Likes

2. She and her family try new foods all the time.

   try

3. One day her dad bought a jar of salsa.

   bought

4. The sauce has tomatoes, onions, and hot peppers in it.

   in

5. The delicious sauce burns her tongue a little.

   burns

×8

B. Choose a simple predicate from the word box to complete each sentence. Then circle the complete predicate.

| chopped | decided | laughed | wiped | squirted |

1. One afternoon Lola *decided* to make salsa.

2. First, she *chopped* the tomatoes into small pieces.

3. The red tomatoes *squirted* juice all over her clothes.

4. Her sister *laughed* at the red juice on Lola's shirt.

5. Lola *wiped* the juice off easily.

×5

C. Write a short passage about a new food you tried. Use complete sentences.

Vanilla or Chocolate?

A. Read the sentences. Draw one line under each complete subject. Draw two lines under each complete predicate. Then circle the simple subject and simple predicate in each sentence.

My brother Jake works in an ice-cream shop. He loves ice cream! Jake tastes all the different flavors. The customers love his tasty ice-cream sundaes. My dad takes me to the shop sometimes.

B. Draw a line to connect each subject on the left to a predicate on the right. Write the complete sentences on the lines.

The small shop   buy ice-cream cones.

Many people   is chocolate.

The most popular flavor   gets busy on weekends.

1. _____

2. _____

3. _____

C. Write a paragraph about your favorite dessert. Include four sentences, and underline the simple subjects and predicates.

A Special Walk

A. Circle *C* if the group of words is a complete sentence. Circle *I* if it is an incomplete sentence.

1. Ramon cares about his street. **C   I**

2. Decides to pick up the litter. **C   I**

3. The people next door. **C   I**

4. He finds a pair of gloves. **C   I**

5. They will keep his hands clean. **C   I**

B. Read each incomplete sentence. Rewrite it as a complete sentence by adding a word or phrase from the chart.

Subject	Predicate
The neighbors	puts the litter in the bag.
Ramon	are on the sidewalk.

1. Two candy wrappers.

_____

2. Grabs a plastic bag.

_____

3. This helpful boy.

_____

4. Greet Ramon with a smile.

_____

C. Write a short passage about something you have done or could do to keep your neighborhood clean. Be sure to use complete sentences.

What a Surprise!

A. Read the passage. Draw a line under each group of words that is not a complete sentence.

Tina woke up early on Saturday. Was a beautiful sunny day.

Tina loved the outdoors. She looked out the window. Saw her

mom's car. She would wash the car for her mom. A clean car.

B. Add a subject or predicate from the chart to make each group of words a complete sentence. Write the new sentences on the lines.

Subject	Predicate
Tina	wanted to help Tina.
Tina and Dan	got a bucket of soapy water.

1. Put on her old T-shirt and shorts.

_____

2. She.

_____

3. Tina's younger brother Dan.

_____

4. Would surprise their mom with a clean car.

_____

_____

C. Write a short passage about a time you tried to surprise someone. Be sure to use complete sentences.

Let It Rain

A. Match each subject to its predicate. Write the new sentences on the lines.

Subject	Predicate
The rain	was a fun movie to watch.
Mia's grandpa	made popcorn together.
Mia	ruined Mia's plans for outdoor fun.
Mia and Grandpa	liked her grandpa's ideas.
The Wizard of Oz	used his pen to list ideas for a rainy day.

1. _____

2. _____

3. _____

4. _____

5. _____

B. Read each word or group of words. Add a subject or predicate. Write the sentence on the line.

1. Mia.

   _____

2. Read the next chapter in her mystery book.

   _____

3. Fell asleep for an hour after that.

   _____

4. Her sister.

   _____

C. Write a paragraph about a rainy-day activity. Use three complete sentences.

Crawly Caterpillars

A. Read each sentence. Decide whether it is a simple sentence (*S*) or a compound sentence (*C*). Write *S* or *C* on the line.

1. A caterpillar has many legs.   _____

2. It can crawl, but it cannot fly.   _____

3. A caterpillar builds a soft shell around itself.   _____

4. The shell protects caterpillars from the wind, and it   _____
   keeps them dry.

5. A caterpillar may be all green, or it may be red   _____
   and yellow.

6. Some caterpillars have smooth skin.   _____

7. Others have bumps all over their skin.   _____

8. A caterpillar changes shape inside its shell, and it   _____
   becomes a butterfly.

B. Complete each compound sentence by adding a comma and a conjunction. Use each conjunction from the word box one time.

and   but   or

1. A caterpillar eats a lot of plants _____ it grows and grows.

2. A caterpillar has twelve eyes _____ it does not have ears.

3. People may love caterpillars _____ they may be afraid of
   these insects.

C. Write a paragraph about caterpillars or butterflies. Use both simple and compound sentences.

Ants: Friends or Enemies?

A. **Read the paragraph. Find the four compound sentences. Draw a line under each one.**

Ants have been on Earth a long time. Ants may live under the ground, or they may live inside trees. Some ants make nests from leaves. Ants live in groups, and they share food. Most ants are very tiny, but some grow to be an inch long. They may be small, but they are strong. An ant can lift things that weigh ten times more than it does. That's one powerful ant!

B. **Complete the paragraph by writing *and, or,* or *but* in each space. Add a comma before each one.**

Many people think ants are pests _____ ants can be helpful. They eat other insects _____ they dig up soil. The digging makes the soil healthier. Sometimes ants bother us. They may get into our houses. They may crawl on our skin. Do you like ants _____ do you think they are pests?

C. **Write a paragraph about whether an ant would make a good pet. Use simple and compound sentences.**

Grasshoppers

A. **Read the paragraph. Find three mistakes with the compound sentences. Cross out each mistake you find, and write the correction above it.**

A grasshopper's body has three parts, or it is covered by a shell. The grasshopper has six legs and it uses all six to walk. Its legs are strong, but the back legs are strongest. The grasshopper uses its powerful back legs to jump. To protect themselves, grasshoppers can jump away, but they can hide in the grass.

B. **Rewrite each pair of sentences to form one compound sentence. Write the new sentences on the lines.**

1. Alonzo's class went to the park. The students looked for grasshoppers.

   _____

   _____

2. Alonzo took his notebook. He left his heavy backpack at school.

   _____

   _____

3. Hannah found a grasshopper in the grass. She pointed it out.

   _____

   _____

4. The students had to be quiet. The grasshopper would hop away.

   _____

   _____

C. **Write a paragraph about a field trip you took with your class. Include four compound sentences.**

A Birthday Party That Pops

A. Read each sentence. Draw one line under the group of words that tells a complete thought. Draw two lines under the group of words that does not tell a complete thought. Circle the conjunction.

1. Grace wakes up early because today is her birthday.

2. She feels excited before she even gets out of bed.

3. Grace counts the hours until her party begins.

4. She starts getting ready after she walks the dog.

B. Connect each sentence on the left to a word group on the right that makes the most sense. Write the new sentences on the lines. Circle the conjunction.

The party could not begin   before Grace shared her cake.

Kids played lots of games   after everyone left.

Grace thanked her mom   until all the guests arrived.

1. _____

   _____

2. _____

   _____

3. _____

   _____

C. Write a short passage about a birthday party you would like to have. Use simple sentences and complex sentences.

The Best Day!

A. Read each sentence. Circle the conjunction that works best. Then write it on the line.

1. Yesterday was Georgio's best day at school _____ he made a new friend. (before, because)

2. Georgio saw Sally _____ she got off of the school bus. (when, until)

3. Sally was scared _____ it was her first day of school. (because, after)

4. Georgio said hello to Sally _____ she got to the school door. (before, until)

5. He brought Sally to the office _____ she didn't know where to go. (after, because)

6. Sally felt better _____ Georgio walked her to her classroom. (after, before)

7. He waited _____ Sally's teacher introduced her to the class. (until, before)

8. Sally thanked Georgio _____ he left for his class. (because, before)

9. Sally didn't think she would like her new school _____ she made a new friend. (because, until)

B. Write a short passage about a time when you helped someone. Use simple sentences and complex sentences.

Grandpa's Present

A. Read the passage. Circle the correct conjunctions.

Avi was worried (because, after) she didn't have a birthday present for her grandpa. She needed to think of something (before, after) tomorrow. What could she get? She didn't have money to buy anything. Avi thought and thought (because, until) she finally came up with an idea. She would write a poem for Grandpa David. Avi drew pictures of Grandpa's favorite things all around the poem (after, until) she had carefully copied it onto shiny paper.

B. Use a conjunction from the word box to combine each sentence pair to form a complex sentence. Write the new sentence on the lines.

after   because   before

1. Avi was a little nervous. Grandpa opened his present.

_____

_____

2. She felt much better. He gave her a big, warm hug.

_____

_____

3. Grandpa David loved his present. No one had ever written a poem for him.

_____

_____

C. Write a short passage about the best present you have given to someone. Include three simple sentences and two complex sentences.

A Family Trip

A. What is needed to make each phrase a complete sentence?
Write S (for *subject*) or P (for *predicate*).

1. Visited San Francisco. _____

2. One of the nicest parks for kids. _____

3. Pours water into a wading pool. _____

4. A big grassy field. _____

5. A giant merry-go-round. _____

B. Read each incomplete sentence. Correct it by adding a subject or predicate. Write the new sentence on the line.

1. Will visit the Space Center this summer.

   _____

2. Stays open at night.

   _____

3. Like the center's outdoor slumber parties.

   _____

4. Helps you look at the stars through a telescope.

   _____

5. My family.

   _____

C. Write a brief passage about a trip you took. Be sure to use complete sentences.

On the Beach

A. Draw a line to connect each simple sentence on the left to a sentence on the right. Add a comma and a conjunction from the word box. Write the sentences on the lines.

and but or

I like to swim in a pool.   I swim with fish at the same time.

I ride the ocean waves.   I can look for seashells in the sand.

I can build sandcastles.   I like the ocean even more.

1. _____

_____

2. _____

_____

3. _____

_____

B. Read each sentence pair. Circle the conjunction at the end of each sentence pair that could be used to combine the sentences correctly.

1. I always put on sunscreen. I go to the beach. (after, before)

2. Dad sets up an umbrella. It offers shade from the sun. (because, until)

3. We swim, play, and read. It gets dark. (after, until)

C. Write a brief passage about something you like to do in the summer. Use simple, compound, and complex sentences.

Space Camp

A. Read the passage. Correct each incomplete sentence.

      Like to go to Space Camp? It's lots of fun. NASA astronauts. Then you train to be an astronaut. Can sit at the controls of the space shuttle. Can try some space exploration activities. Kids ages 14 and older. Kids from ages 7 to 13 can attend a half-day training program.

B. Read each incomplete sentence. Add a subject or a predicate to complete it.

1. A journey into space.

    _____

2. Visitors at the Space Center.

    _____

3. Strap in to a make-believe shuttle.

    _____

4. People of all ages.

    _____

C. Write a passage about what you imagine being in space might be like.
Use complete sentences.

The Walls Around Me

A. Read each sentence. Circle the two nouns in each one. Then underline the noun that is plural.

1. My parents stared at my bedroom.

2. The paintings on the wall were old.

3. My brother said to draw puppies.

4. A forest with deer is also interesting.

5. My sister said to paint different shapes.

B. Circle the noun that correctly completes each sentence. Write the noun on the line.

1. My friend Beth said to draw men and _____ in a circus. (womans, women)

2. Then I thought about painting _____ with colorful wings. (butterflys, butterflies)

3. I could also draw _____ and then count them at night. (sheeps, sheep)

4. There were so many _____ to paint the walls! (ways, wayes)

5. Finally, I just picked up one of the _____ and started to paint. (brushs, brushes)

C. Write a paragraph about what you would paint on the walls of a bedroom. Use singular and plural nouns.

Making a Mural

A. Circle the *S* if the underlined noun is singular and the *P* if it is plural.

1. The fourth graders are making a <u>mural</u> about their community.   **S**   **P**

2. The <u>children</u> talk about what to include in the mural.   **S**   **P**

3. They decide to show some important <u>buildings</u>.   **S**   **P**

4. They want to include their new school <u>bus</u>.   **S**   **P**

5. They also want to show <u>geese</u> sitting near the lake.   **S**   **P**

B. Choose the nouns from the chart that correctly complete the story. Write the nouns on the lines.

Singular	crayon	bench	man	baby	paper
Plural	crayons	benches	men	babies	papers

The students plan to draw children of all ages,

including _____. They will also include

_____ and women who work in the community.

They will show parks with _____ so people can

sit. First, the students will draw their picture in pencil on the

mural, which is made of _____. Then they will

use _____ to add bright colors.

C. Write a short passage about a drawing or painting. Use singular and plural nouns.

Welcome Home, Welcome Home!

A. Proofread the passage. Cross out each incorrect singular or plural noun. Write the correct form of the noun above it.

Aunt Li came home from the hospital today with her two

twin babys. We made a big banners that said, "Welcome Home!"

It was six feets long. We decorated it with pictures of

little bears, foxs, and other baby animals. Then we made some

sandwichies for everyone in the family to eat.

B. Replace each singular noun with its plural form. Write the new sentence on the line.

1. We heard the car <u>door</u> shut.

   _____

2. Aunt Li walked in, and all the <u>child</u> ran up to her.

   _____

3. "I hope you are not giving <u>speech</u> today," she said.

   _____

4. Instead, my brother gave Aunt Li two stuffed <u>sheep</u> for her girls.

   _____

5. Aunt Li thanked us and said, "I love homecoming <u>party</u>."

   _____

C. Write a paragraph about a fun way to welcome someone home. Use three singular and two plural nouns.

Hats, Feathers, and Pirates

A. Read the sentences. Underline the common nouns. Circle the proper nouns. You should mark three words or groups of words in each sentence.

1. My mom works for the Cookoo Costume Company in Springtown.

2. Arthur Featherman, who moved here from Canada, owns the shop.

3. My mother once made a hat that looked like the Statue of Liberty.

4. Her costumes for Thanksgiving are very popular in November.

5. Robin Hawke, a friend, just bought a special shirt.

B. Read the passage. Underline the common nouns. Circle the proper nouns.

My friend went to Maysville Costume Museum on June 12. That was the day it opened. Last Friday my whole family went there. The museum has amazing costumes. Some clothes belonged to pirates, such as Davey Doolittle. His jacket was covered with bright feathers. Doolittle lived on an island near Florida. The Doolittle Bridge got its name from another person— not from Davey. Would you want to go across a bridge named after a pirate?

C. Write a paragraph about a place you would like to visit. Use common nouns and proper nouns. Include people, places, and things.

A Holiday for Trees

A. Read the sentences. Circle the correct form of the nouns.

1. People plant trees on a holiday called arbor day.

   Arbor Day
   Arbor day

2. A man named j. sterling morton started the holiday.

   j. Sterling Morton
   J. Sterling Morton

3. He was from detroit, Michigan.

   detroit, Michigan
   Detroit, Michigan

4. He moved to a part of the state of nebraska that had no trees.

   State of Nebraska
   state of Nebraska

5. The first Arbor Day was on friday, April 10, 1872.

   Friday, April
   friday, April

B. Read the sentences and underline the proper nouns. Circle the words at the end of the sentences that tell what the proper nouns name.

1. The students at Goodmont Elementary School learned all about trees. (person, place)

2. The fourth-grade teacher, Mrs. Chen, brought in books about trees. (thing, person)

3. The students went to Golden Leaf Park to learn about different kinds of trees. (place, thing)

4. They made pictures of trees for the Spring Art Show. (person, thing)

5. The mayor of Maplewood came to the school to see all of the art. (person, place)

C. Write a paragraph about a project that took place at your school. Use common nouns and proper nouns.

Small Towns, Big Things

A. Proofread the paragraph. Find five mistakes with common and proper nouns. Cross out each mistake and write the correction above it.

   Many small Towns have interesting things to see. Some have big sculptures made of wood and plastic. One town has a huge statue called the *World's largest Crayon*. It is in Easton, pennsylvania. It was built in october 2003. My family visited it last year. My cousins Freda and dale came with us.

B. Underline the common nouns and circle the proper nouns. Rewrite each sentence on the line, using capital letters correctly.

1. Many people visit North carolina.

   _____

2. Some visitors go to see The coffee Pot.

   _____

3. That famous site is in Winston-Salem.

   _____

4. My friend visited the City last Sunday.

   _____

5. It was the weekend of memorial Day.

   _____

C. Write a paragraph about an unusual object you have seen or read about. Use five proper nouns.

Clean-up Day

A. Read the sentences. Circle the possessive nouns. Circle *S* if the possessive noun is singular and *P* if it is plural.

1. My brother's friends are cleaning up the park.   S   P

2. The park clean-up was Bess's idea.   S   P

3. The friends' plan is to pick up trash.   S   P

4. The park's lawn is covered with litter.   S   P

5. The children's playground needs more trash cans.   S   P

B. Read the paragraph. Underline the singular possessive nouns. Circle the plural possessive nouns.

The friends eat their lunches at the lake's edge. They watch baby geese swim in the water. They listen to the birds' songs. Then they are back to work. They find a person's camera on the ground. Suddenly, they hear women's voices. The women are searching for a lost camera. The friends are glad the camera's owner has returned.

C. Write a paragraph about your favorite park. Use singular and plural possessive nouns.

Putting on a Play

A. Read each sentence. Circle the possessive noun that correctly completes it. Then write the word on the line.

1. _____ friends decided to put on a play. (Leahs', Leah's)

2. They used the community _____ basement for their show. (centers, center's)

3. They had to move the _____ furniture to set up a stage. (room's, rooms)

4. My mom sewed the _____ costumes. (children's, childrens')

5. The kids borrowed some fun hats from _____ grandfather. (Ross's, Rosses)

6. They found umbrellas and other things in a _____ attic. (neighbors, neighbor's)

7. The _____ families came to see the play. (actors', actors)

8. The _____ cheers proved that the play was a success. (audiences, audience's)

B. Write a short passage about a play you took part in or went to see. Use singular and plural possessive nouns.

Save the Library!

A. Proofread the passage. Cross out each incorrect form of a possessive noun. Write the correct form of the possessive noun above it.

Tammys class loves going to the library. The librarys' rooms

are filled with exciting books. Now the city's leaders want to close

the library. They say there is not enough money to keep it open.

The librarians have asked for the communities help. They want

the childrens' help, too. The kids could make posters to show how

important the library is to them. All of the students's posters

could make a difference.

B. Replace each underlined phrase with the correct possessive noun. Then write the sentence on the line.

1. The <u>signs belonging to the kids</u> were put in stores and parks.

   _____

2. <u>The poster belonging to Tammy</u> was read by hundreds of people.

   _____

3. The <u>posters made by the children</u> helped to keep the library open.

   _____

C. Write a paragraph about a library you have visited. Use four possessive nouns.

The Spinner

A. Read the sentences. Circle the subject pronouns.

1. Gil read a book about dog tricks. He decided to teach an old dog a new trick.

2. Gil's friends were excited. They wanted to make a video of the dog.

3. Gil's sister wondered if the dog could learn tricks. She had heard that old dogs can't learn new tricks.

4. Gil said to his sister Rita, "You just wait. I can teach this dog anything!"

B. Read the sentences. Circle the object pronouns.

1. Gil got some dog treats and put them in his pocket.

2. He called the dog over to him.

3. Gil pulled out a treat, and the dog sniffed it.

4. Gil moved the treat in a circle, again and again. The dog followed it.

5. "Look! The dog is spinning in circles!" Gil cried out. "The two of us are a real team!"

6. "I told you I could teach Spinner to spin!" Gil said to Rita.

C. Write a short passage about an animal trick you have seen. Use two subject pronouns and two object pronouns.

Misty's Eyes

A. Read each sentence. Circle the pronoun that correctly completes it. Then write the pronoun on the line.

1. My friend Rana and _____ met a dog that was blind. (I, me)

2. _____ saw the dog at a neighborhood picnic. (Us, We)

3. Rana saw _____ first. (it, them)

4. _____ ran over to talk to the dog's owner, Mr. Moore. (She, Her)

5. "Do you want to pet Misty?" _____ asked. (him, he)

6. The two of _____ gently patted the dog's head. (we, us)

7. Then Rana showed _____ another dog, standing nearby. (me, I)

8. "Do _____ know what this pup can do?" Mr. Moore asked. (you, her)

9. We watched as _____ picked up Misty's leash and led the dog around. (them, it)

10. Rana and I exclaimed, "_____ are amazing!" (They, Them)

B. Write a short passage about an amazing animal. Use two subject pronouns and two object pronouns.

Catch Me If You Can

A. Proofread the passage. Cross out the five incorrect pronouns and write the correct pronouns above them.

Nick and his dog Pepito played in the park. Them both got muddy. Back at home, Nick's mom told he to take a bath. Her also said Pepito needed a bath. "We should wash Pepito first," Nick said.

Pepito does not like bath time, so him ran away. "Pepito, come back to I right now!" shouted Nick.

B. Read the passage. Replace the underlined words with pronouns to make the sentences sound smoother. Write each pronoun above the underlined word or words.

Nick found Pepito. <u>Nick</u> grabbed the dog by the collar. <u>The collar</u> came off. The dog ran away again and knocked into the table. Two lamps fell over. Luckily, <u>the lamps</u> did not break. Nick picked <u>the lamps</u> up. The boy finally caught the dog and put it in the tub. Pepito splashed water all over <u>the boy</u>. At least Pepito was having fun!

C. Write a short passage about caring for a pet or animal. Use the pronouns *I, me, it, they,* and *them.*

Owls in the Night

A. **Read the sentences. Circle the possessive pronoun in each sentence.**

1. Owls are one of my favorite animals.

2. My mom likes all kinds of birds, especially the owl.

3. We went out at night to look for owls near our house.

4. We wanted to find their nests.

5. We took Dad's camera because Mom couldn't find hers.

B. **Read the passage. Circle each possessive pronoun.**

After about an hour, Mom and I spotted an owl. Its nest was in the hole of a tree. Mom took the camera out of her pocket and snapped a picture. Then it was my turn to take a photo. I looked right into the owl's eyes. It stared back into mine. The owl seemed to wink. I took a bunch of pictures. Later we showed our photos to Dad.

"Yours are a real hoot, Vanessa!" he said.

C. **Write a short passage about a real or make-believe animal that comes out at night. Use at least three possessive pronouns.**

To the Lighthouse

A. Read each sentence. Circle the possessive pronoun that correctly completes it. Then write the pronoun on the line.

1. Tanya goes on a lot of hikes with _____ dad. (her, his)

2. She says, "_____ favorite hike is to the lighthouse." (Mine, My)

3. The lighthouse is on a hill, and _____ light flashes all night. (its, his)

4. The light helps sailors keep _____ boats away from rocky shores. (theirs, their)

5. On Friday evening, Tanya's dad says, "Let's leave for _____ hike in an hour." (our, her)

6. "Put an extra sweater in _____ backpack," he reminds Tanya. (your, yours)

7. Then he adds, "I already put flashlights and water in _____." (my, mine)

8. "_____ will be really heavy," Tanya says to her father. (Yours, Your)

9. Tanya and her dad follow the trail to _____ end. (its, their)

10. On a quiet night, the lighthouse seems like it is all _____. (their, theirs)

B. Write a short passage about your favorite place. Use at least four possessive pronouns.

Fireflies and Frogs

A. Proofread the passage. Cross out each incorrect possessive pronoun. Write the correct possessive pronoun above it.

A firefly is an insect. Our body has a part that flashes light. Often parents and your children go outside at night to see the fireflies. Jonah likes to go to its neighbor's backyard to watch the fireflies with Clare. One friendly firefly lands on Clare's arm. Another lands on Jonah's hand. "Wow," Jonah says. "Yours firefly is bright." He adds, "It is a lot brighter than his!"

B. Read the sentences. Then choose a possessive pronoun from the word box to complete each one. Write the pronoun on the line.

his   its   their   her   mine

1. Jonah and Clare went to a pond near _____ school to look for frogs.

2. Clare took _____ cell phone to record the frogs' sounds.

3. Jonah wore _____ rain boots in case the ground was muddy.

4. "I wish I had worn _____," Clare said.

5. Clare forgot about her wet feet when she saw a frog and heard _____ croaking sound.

C. Write a paragraph about a fun adventure you have had with a friend. Use five possessive pronouns.

Trash, You Say?

A. Read the sentences. Circle each pronoun. Then circle *C* if the pronoun correctly matches the underlined noun. Circle *I* if the pronoun is incorrect.

1. <u>Gerald</u> took a walk in his neighborhood.   C   I

2. <u>The boy</u> carried a big bag with her.   C   I

3. Gerald found a <u>plastic bag</u> on the ground and put   C   I
   it in the bag.

4. Three <u>paper clips</u> sat on the sidewalk, and Gerald   C   I
   grabbed they, too.

5. A friend asked <u>Gerald</u>, "What are you going to do   C   I
   with these things?"

B. Read the sentences. Circle the noun that each underlined pronoun refers to. Then circle *S* if the pronoun is singular. Circle *P* if the pronoun is plural.

1. Gerald collects things so <u>he</u> can make little   S   P
   animals.

2. Paper clips become insects. Old twist ties become   S   P
   <u>their</u> legs.

3. Gerald hangs up the plastic bag. <u>It</u> looks like a   S   P
   jellyfish.

4. Gerald's friends love the art. <u>They</u> start to collect   S   P
   trash, too.

5. Gerald's parents proudly say, "<u>Our</u> son turns trash   S   P
   into art!"

C. Write a short passage about something you might make from trash. Use three pronouns. Make sure they match the nouns they are replacing.

Lost and Found

A. Read the sentences. Circle the pronoun that correctly refers to the underlined noun or nouns. Write the pronoun on the line.

1. <u>Molli</u> is looking for a sweatshirt in _____ closet. (her, their)

2. Sweaters are piled up on the closet floor. Molli has tossed _____ there. (they, them)

3. Old shoes sit in another pile. <u>Molli</u> says, "Some of these shoes aren't even _____." (his, mine)

4. Some <u>toys</u> sit in a dark corner of the closet. _____ broke somehow. (It, They)

5. The <u>sweatshirt</u> Molli is looking for is red. _____ has a hood. (It, She)

6. "_____ can't find anything in this closet," <u>Molli</u> thinks to herself. (We, I)

7. Finally, the <u>girl</u> finds the sweatshirt. _____ puts it on. (Her, She)

8. Just then Molli's sister, Hannah, walks in. "What are _____ doing with that sweatshirt, <u>Molli</u>?" Hannah asks. (you, they)

9. Hannah tells <u>Molli</u>, "That sweatshirt isn't _____!" (yours, his)

10. Hannah adds, "I've been looking for that <u>sweatshirt</u> for weeks! Thanks for finding _____." (it, them)

B. Write a short passage describing a closet in your home or at school. Use three pronouns. Make sure that each one matches the noun it is replacing.

A Lucky Day

A. Read the paragraph. Find six pronouns that are used incorrectly. Cross out each one and write the correct pronoun above it.

     Dan looks out the window at the first snow of winter. He is excited to go out and play. Dan grabs her scarf, mittens, and warm jacket. Dan's dad tells them to wear a warm hat, too. Suddenly, Dan feels something in its jacket pocket. He finds a small wooden eagle. She was a gift from Grandfather. Dan yells out, "You found the eagle! This is really their lucky day!"

B. Read the sentences. Complete each sentence by writing the correct pronoun on the line.

1. Dan wants to put _____ eagle somewhere safe.

2. Dan's sister, Lily, shows _____ a safe place for the eagle.

3. Lily has put some special things there, and _____ have stayed safe.

4. "What happens if _____ forget where the safe place is?" Dan asks.

5. "Then you will just have to ask _____," Dan's sister says, smiling.

C. Write a paragraph about a safe place to keep your favorite things. Use four pronouns. Make sure that each matches the noun it is replacing.

Fairy Tales

A. Complete each sentence. Write the plural form of the word in parentheses.

1. Fairy _____ are make-believe stories. (tale)

2. Sometimes a character is granted three _____. (wish)

3. Tattered _____ turn into beautiful ball gowns. (dress)

4. Pumpkins become golden _____. (coach)

5. Horses appear where _____ once stood. (mouse)

6. Country girls get to dance with _____. (prince)

7. Do you like these _____? Do you wish they could come true? (story)

B. Underline the common nouns. Circle the proper nouns.

1. girl
2. Dorothy
3. land
4. Oz
5. dog
6. Toto
7. friend
8. Scarecrow
9. Wicked Witch
10. enemy
11. home
12. Kansas

C. Write a brief passage about your favorite fairy tale or story. Use singular, plural, common, and proper nouns.

After-school Fun

A. Complete each sentence. Use the correct subject pronoun for the word or words in parentheses.

You He She It We

1. _____ want to start a crafts club at school.
   (My friends and I)

2. _____ would teach us how to make puppets.
   (Mrs. Burrell)

3. _____ would teach us to build models with wood.
   (Mr. Moore)

4. _____ would offer two new crafts every year.
   (The crafts club)

B. Read the passage. Replace the underlined words with an object pronoun in the word box. Write it above the words.

me you him her it us them

My family went to Margie's Pizza Place. My dad told

the server that we wanted an extra large mushroom pie. She

suggested to my family and me that we add broccoli and

peppers. "The price includes three toppings!" she said.

"That sounds like a delicious pizza!" my dad said. My

family decided to order the pizza with three toppings.

C. Write a brief passage about something you like to do with your friends or family. Use subject and object pronouns in your passage.

The Great Outdoors

A. Read the passage. Find and circle four possessive nouns. Write *S* above each singular possessive noun and *P* above each plural possessive noun.

The clouds' gray darkness began to fill the sky. The seagulls' squawks pierced through the growing wind. The beach's salty air was lifting blankets off of the sand. A storm was coming in. Our family's picnic would have to move indoors. Luckily, my grandma has a house near the shore.

B. Rewrite each sentence. Replace the underlined words with a possessive pronoun.

1. <u>My family's</u> hiking trip will take place this spring.

   _____

2. <u>Dad's</u> dream has been to visit Yosemite National Park.

   _____

3. There is wildlife everywhere along <u>Yosemite's</u> trails.

   _____

4. I am going to use <u>Mom's</u> camera for the first time.

   _____

C. Write a brief passage about a place you would like to visit and what you would bring on the trip. Use four possessive nouns and three possessive pronouns.

Polar Bears

A. Read the passage. Circle each action verb.

Polar bears live in the cold north. They hunt seals on the ice. A polar bear also swims. Its big front paws pull it through the water. A thick layer of fat protects the bear from the cold.

B. Read the sentences. Write *H* above each helping verb. Write *M* above each main verb.

A polar bear can smell a seal on the ice 20 miles away! The bear can also find seals through holes in the ice. A seal may pop up for air. If a seal does come up, the polar bear will grab it. Polar bears have survived this way for a long time.

C. Make up a story about a polar bear. Write a paragraph about what the bear does. Use at least three verbs.

Grizzly Bears

A. Read the paragraph. Write a verb from the word box on each line. Use each verb only once.

have	digs	sleep	eat	live	catch	will	do	keeps	run

Grizzly bears _____ in Alaska, Canada, and other

places. These giant bears _____ both plants and meat.

Some grizzlies _____ fish in streams. Others _____

eat animals as big as moose!

A grizzly bear _____ a den, or hole, for the winter.

The bear will _____ there all winter long. The den also

_____ baby bears, or cubs, safe.

Grizzly bears are huge, and they can _____ very

fast. I _____ seen many pictures of grizzly bears. But I

_____ not want to meet one in person!

B. Make up a story about an animal that lives in the woods. Write a short paragraph about it. Use at least four verbs.

Bear-y Hungry

A. Read the passage. Circle the action verb in each sentence. Underline the helping verb, if there is one.

A big bear has crawled out of its den. The bear yawns.

Then its stomach growls. The bear does not see any food.

Maybe it can find some nearby.

B. Write a verb from the word box to complete each sentence.

have	holds	chew	grows	can

1. A panda bear _____ eat a lot of bamboo.

2. Its strong teeth can _____ the tough plant.

3. The panda _____ the stems with its fingers.

4. The bamboo plant that pandas eat _____ in China.

5. Bamboo forests _____ grown for millions of years.

C. Write a short passage about what you eat. Use five verbs, including two helping verbs.

My Aunt and Uncle

A. Read the passage. Circle each linking verb. If it has a helping verb, write _H_ above the helping verb.

My uncle and aunt are both artists. Uncle Victor is a painter.

He paints pictures of animals and plants. The pictures look very

realistic. Aunt Carmen carves pretty bowls out of wood. They feel

smooth and soft.

Aunt Carmen and Uncle Victor have been together since

college. They met each other in art class. At first they were

friends. Then they married. Next Saturday will be their tenth

anniversary.

B. Describe something you have made. Use at least three linking verbs.

Picture This

A. Read each sentence. Circle the linking verb that completes the sentence. Write the verb on the line.

1. I _____ a good artist. (are, am)

2. The drawing of the sunset _____ pretty. (was, were)

3. Be careful! That paint _____ wet. (is, am)

4. My uncle _____ an artist for ten years. (have be, has been)

5. I _____ happy when I finish my drawing. (will be, were)

B. Write a verb from the word box to complete each sentence. Use each verb only once.

smells   looks   feels

1. The art room _____ messy.

2. The ball of clay _____ soft and wet.

3. The paint _____ stinky.

C. Describe your classroom. Use at least four linking verbs.

Art Everywhere!

A. Read the passage. Circle each verb. If it is a linking verb, write *L* above it. If it is an action verb, write *A* above it.

My school is near the art museum. Last week my class went to the museum. Each room was full of beautiful art objects. We looked at many paintings and drawings. Some pictures seemed very old. Others were newer. We learned interesting facts about each one.

B. Write three sentences. Choose a subject, a linking verb, and the word or words that go best with the subject.

Subject	Linking Verb	Words That Tell About the Subject
I	feels	in the paint
The glue	were	sticky
The brushes	am	a good writer

1. _____

   _____

2. _____

   _____

3. _____

   _____

C. Describe a work of art that you have seen or made. It can be a drawing, a painting, a photograph, a statue, or a mural on a wall. Use five linking verbs to tell about it.

To the Moon

A. Read the passage. Write *present*, *past*, or *future* above each underlined verb.

On July 20, 1969, two astronauts <u>landed</u> on the moon.

Neil Armstrong <u>stepped</u> out first. Buzz Aldrin <u>followed</u> him.

People back on Earth <u>cheered</u>!

Today astronauts from many countries <u>work</u> in space.

They <u>live</u> together in a big station. They <u>study</u> the stars and

planets up close.

Maybe someday you <u>will live</u> in space. Or maybe you

<u>will walk</u> on the moon!

B. Read each sentence. Circle the correct form of the verb.

1. Neil Armstrong (will walk, walked) on the moon in 1969.

2. Next week my class (will visit, visited) the Space Museum.

3. In the past, rockets (blasted, blast) astronauts into space.

4. Today astronauts (traveled, travel) on a space shuttle.

C. Make up a story about going to the moon. Use the past, present, and future tenses in your writing.

The Stinky Planet

A. Read the story. Use verbs from the word box to complete it. Make sure you write the correct form to show past, present, or future. Remember to write the word *will* before each future-tense verb.

save shout wait smell open look walk need

James and Julia peeked out the window of the spaceship.

"Wow!" Julia _____. "Look at this planet!" She

went to the door. She slowly _____ it. Then she

_____ down the steps.

James was afraid to go with her. "I _____

here," he said.

Julia sniffed the air. "I _____ something

funny," she said. Then she _____ at the ground.

She was stuck in brown goo. "James, help! I _____

you right now!"

"Don't worry!" James said. "I _____ you!"

B. Write about what happens next to James and Julia. Use the past, present, and future tenses correctly.

Space Is the Place

A. Complete the chart. Fill in the missing verbs.

Present	Past	Future
wait	waited	_____
walk	_____	will walk
_____	landed	will land
learn	learned	_____
_____	looked	will look

B. Read each sentence. Circle the correct verb to complete the sentence. Write it on the line.

1. In 1942 the first rocket _____ into space.

   (zoomed, will zoom)

2. Today computers _____ astronauts in space.

   (help, helped)

3. Last night I _____ up at the stars.

   (gazed, will gaze)

4. Maybe someday people _____ on Mars.

   (live, will live)

C. Pretend you are lost in space. How did you get there? What will you do? Write six sentences, and use the past, present, and future tenses correctly.

Moving Land

A. Read the passage. Underline the past-tense verbs.

Mountains are tall landforms. They are formed in different

ways. The Rocky Mountains formed millions of years ago.

Earth's crust moved, and big pieces of land pushed into each

other. Slowly, one piece slipped under the other. The land rose

up. It became a string of mountains. These mountains now

stretch from Canada to New Mexico. Maybe mountains will form

somewhere else someday.

B. Read each sentence. Circle the correct form of the verb.

1. Yesterday people in Japan (felt, feeled) a small earthquake.

2. The ground (rockked, rocked) for a few seconds.

3. Buildings (shakeed, shook), but nothing (break, broke).

4. The quake (stopped, stoped). Life (goed, went) back to normal.

C. Imagine you felt the earth move. What happened? Write about it. Use at least three past-tense verbs.

The Volcano

A. Read the passage. Find each underlined verb. Write its past-tense form above it.

Akahi <u>live</u> on the island of Hawaii. One day when he was

little, he was outside on his bike. He <u>look</u> up at a faraway

mountain. A cloud of smoke <u>float</u> above it.

His heart <u>skip</u> a beat. He <u>feel</u> afraid. He <u>hop</u> on his bike

and <u>race</u> home. "Mom! The mountain is on fire!" he said.

Akahi's mother <u>hurry</u> outside. She <u>smile</u>. "The mountain

is not on fire. It is a volcano," she said. "It <u>form</u> long ago. Hot,

melted rock <u>come</u> out of an opening at the top of the mountain.

The melted rock <u>run</u> down the sides. Then it <u>cool</u>. But the inside

of the mountain is still hot. Sometimes steam comes out of the

top. That is what you saw."

B. Write the beginning of a story about a boy or a girl who visits a volcano. Use at least four past-tense verbs.

Rock and Roll

A. Complete the chart. Fill in the missing verb forms.

Present	Past
stop	_____
_____	moved
_____	went
feel	_____
_____	rubbed
hurry	_____

B. Proofread the paragraph. Cross out each incorrect past-tense form and write the correct form above it.

One day a rock falled off a cliff. It droped on the ground.

When it landed, it breaked into smaller rocks. Over time the

rocks becomed even smaller. They turn to bits of sand.

C. Pretend you are a rock that formed long ago. What happened to you? Use at least four past-tense verbs.

Sunflower Seeds

A. Read each sentence. Underline the simple subject. Then circle the correct form of the verb.

1. Mrs. Ming (grows, grow) sunflowers.

2. The sunflowers (gets, get) very tall.

3. Each flower (has, have) bright yellow petals.

4. The seeds (are, am) in the center of the flower.

5. Sometimes Mrs. Ming (dry, dries) the seeds.

6. She (have, has) given me some to eat.

7. You (cracks, crack) the shell with your teeth.

8. The seed inside (is, are) tiny but tasty.

9. I (am, is) helping Mrs. Ming this afternoon.

10. We (are, is) collecting seeds from flowers.

B. Write five sentences about making or eating a healthy snack. Make sure each verb agrees with its subject. Use at least three of these verbs: *am, is, are, has,* or *have.*

Plant Parts

A. Read the story. Write a verb from the word box to complete each sentence. Add an ending to the verb if it needs one.

make   know   hold   carry   drink

I _____ the main parts of a plant.

The roots are at the bottom. They _____ water

from the ground. The stem _____ up the plant.

It also _____ water to the leaves. The leaves

_____ food from the water and the sun.

B. Read the sentences. Write a helping verb from the word box to complete each sentence.

am   is   are   have   has

1. I _____ learning about seeds in school.

2. We _____ growing lima beans.

3. Most of the seeds _____ sprouted.

4. My seedling _____ getting bigger.

5. It _____ grown a tiny leaf.

C. Write four sentences about the parts of a plant. Make sure each verb agrees with its subject. Use at least three of these verbs: *am, is, are, has,* or *have.*

Lions and Bees

A. Proofread the passage. Cross out any verb that does not agree with its subject. Write the correct form of the verb above it.

I sees a pretty flower. It are growing next to the sidewalk.

It have a long stem with leaves at the bottom. The flower has

little yellow petals. They forms a circle around the center. It look

like a lion's mane! It is a dandelion.

B. Write the correct verb from the word box to complete each sentence.

fly lands flower flies flowers land

One bee _____ around the pink flower. Three bees

_____ around the red flower. The _____ smell

sweet. One _____ smells the sweetest. A bee _____

on it. Soon the other bees _____ there, too.

C. Imagine you are a bee. What do you see and do? Write at least four sentences. Use a different verb in each sentence. Make sure each verb agrees with its subject.

Shooting Hoops

A. Write a verb from the word box to complete each sentence. Use each verb only once. Add an ending to the verb if it needs one.

catch	wave	throw	jump	bounce	try

Jessica _____ the ball to Josh. He

_____ the ball. He _____ it

twice on the floor. Two players _____ to steal

the ball from him. They _____ their arms.

They _____ up and down.

B. Read the passage. Circle each helping verb. Draw an arrow from the helping verb to its main verb.

Josh looks at the basket. He will score two points

if the ball goes in. Can he do it? Finally he throws. He

does not miss. *Swish*! The ball has dropped through the net.

C. Write about playing your favorite sport. Use at least three action verbs, and include at least one helping verb.

Football, Outside and In

A. Read the passage. Circle each linking verb. Include the helping verb if it has one.

A football field is big. It is 100 yards long. Most football fields are outside. But they can be inside, too. They may be under a big dome. The grass is fake, but it looks and feels almost real. The Superdome is in New Orleans. I saw a game there once. It was fun! I have been a fan ever since.

B. Circle the correct form of the linking verb to complete each sentence. Then write it on the line.

1. My brother _____ on the football team. (is, are)

2. He _____ the kicker for two years.
   (have be, has been)

3. I _____ too young to play. (is, am)

4. Someday I _____ old enough. (will be, will been)

C. Write about a place where you like to play. Use at least three linking verbs, and include at least one helping verb.

Soccer Saturday

A. Proofread the story. Cross out each incorrect verb form. Write the correct form above it.

Last Saturday I go to a soccer game. The Sharks played against the Bobcats. The Bobcats will score three points, but the Sharks was better. They kick four goals. The Sharks always wins. Next Saturday they will face the Hawks. The Hawks lose, probably.

B. Complete the chart. Fill in the missing verbs.

Present	Past	Future
throw	threw	_____
drop	_____	will drop
_____	jumped	will jump
come	_____	will come

C. Write a story about an exciting game you have seen. Include at least four verbs. Use the past, present, and future tenses correctly.

Perfect Pie

A. Read the story. Circle each adjective. Draw an arrow to the noun or pronoun it tells about.

Jack made the perfect pie. The crust was crispy and golden. The inside was filled with sweet, juicy fruit. He had used some peaches and three apples. They were red.

Jack left the pie on the table. Later he heard a loud crash. He ran in and found a big, terrible mess. His dog, Roxy, was lapping up his wonderful pie!

B. Read each sentence. Look at the underlined adjective. What does it describe? Circle the answer.

1. I would like a <u>big</u> piece of pie. (how many, how much, what size)

2. We need <u>three</u> forks. (how many, how much, what size)

3. There is <u>no</u> pie left. (how many, how much, what size)

C. Pretend you are making a cake or a pie. Write three sentences telling what you put in it. Use an adjective in each sentence.

Tricks with Treats

A. Read each sentence. Circle the adjective that best completes it. Then write the adjective on the line.

1. We made a gingerbread house with _____ walls. (round, four)

2. We used _____ pieces of candy for bricks. (square, loud)

3. We covered the roof with _____ frosting. (few, green)

4. I sprinkled _____ sugar on it to look like snow. (some, six)

B. Write an adjective from the word box to complete each sentence.

| creamy long one salty funny |

I like food that tastes sweet and _____.

Sometimes I cut a banana into _____ slices.

Then I spread _____ peanut butter on each

slice. Next, I place _____ or two pretzels on

top. It may sound _____, but it's good!

C. Invent a silly snack. Write four sentences about it. Use a different adjective in each sentence.

Pepper Popcorn

A. Read the story. Write a word from the word box on each line.

crunchy two spicy round much

Clara made _____ bags of popcorn. She emptied the

bags into a _____ bowl. The popcorn was _____,

but it didn't have _____ taste. So she added pepper to

make it _____.

B. Read the adjectives in the word box. Write the adjective that answers each question. Use each word only once.

squeaky cold nine white bitter

1. Which word tells how something can feel? _____

2. Which word tells how something can sound? _____

3. Which word tells how something can look? _____

4. Which word tells how something can taste? _____

5. Which word tells how many? _____

C. What do you like to eat? Write about it. Use at least five different adjectives in your description.

How to Get There

A. Read each sentence. Circle the correct form of the adjective. Write it on the line.

1. There are three ways to get to school, but one is the
_____. (easier, easiest)

2. Oak Drive is much _____ than First Street.
(nicer, nicest)

3. First Street has a lot of cars, but it is _____ than
Oak Drive. (shorter, shortest)

4. Carter Road has the _____ cars, and it is easy to
find. (fewer, fewest)

5. I think Carter Road is the _____ way to go.
(better, best)

B. Read the paragraph. Circle each adjective. Write *1* above each adjective that compares one thing to another thing. Write *2* above each adjective that compares one thing to two or more things.

The street I live on is a steep road. However, the street to

my school is steeper. The school is at the top of a tall hill. It is

the tallest hill in the city. Once I rode my bike to the top. The

way down was easier than the way up! I'm glad I take the bus to

school. That is the best way to go. It is more comfortable than

my bike.

C. Write three sentences about the best way to get to your school. Use adjectives that compare the different streets or types of transportation.

A Good Day for Boating

A. Read the first sentence in each group. Write the correct form of the underlined adjective to complete the other two sentences.

1. Captain Breeze took his sailboat out on a <u>windy</u> day.

   It was _____ than the day before.

   It was the _____ day that week.

2. "Today is a <u>good</u> day for sailing," thought Captain Breeze.

   "It is _____ than yesterday."

   "It is the _____ day this week."

3. A fisherman passed by in a <u>small</u> rowboat.

   It was _____ than the sailboat.

   The rowboat was the _____ of all the boats on the lake.

4. The fisherman shouted, "The sky is <u>beautiful</u> today, isn't it?"

   "Yes!" Captain Breeze shouted back. "It is even _____ than yesterday."

   "I think this is the _____ weather we have had all year."

B. Write four sentences about the weather this week. Use adjectives to compare the weather on different days.

Flying High

A. Proofread the story. Cross out each incorrect adjective. Write the correct form of the adjective above it.

I saw two airplanes in the sky. One was a jet. It was highest

than the other plane. It was also biger. Then a third airplane flew

by. It was the small plane of the three. It was also the slower of

all. However, it was the more colorful plane I have ever seen.

B. Complete the chart. Fill in the missing adjectives.

One	Compared to Another	Compared to Two or More
strong	stronger	_____
_____	heavier	heaviest
thin	thinner	_____
good	better	_____
important	_____	most important

C. Write five sentences about things you might see in the sky. Use adjectives to compare them. Use *better* or *best* at least once.

Penny and Copper

A. Read the story. Circle each adverb. Underline the verb that it tells about.

Princess Penny sat sadly by her castle window. She

was a happy girl, but today she cried. Her favorite horse,

Copper, had disappeared. Penny missed him terribly.

Suddenly, she heard a noise. She looked outside and

saw Copper. "You're back!" she shouted joyfully. She ran

downstairs and hugged him tightly.

B. Read each sentence. Circle the adverb. Write whether it tells *how*, *where*, or *when*.

1. Penny gently stroked Copper's mane.   _____

2. Penny rode Copper around.   _____

3. Later they returned to the barn.   _____

C. Where do you think Penny's horse went the day before? Write at least three sentences about it. Use three adverbs to tell how, where, and when.

Across the River

A. Write the adverb from the word box that means the opposite of the underlined adverb in each sentence. Then reread the sentences.

later carefully early lightly slowly brightly

1. Penny and her horse left the castle <u>late</u> one day. _____

2. The princess sat <u>heavily</u> on Copper's back. _____

3. Copper <u>quickly</u> trotted along the stone path. _____

4. They reached the bridge and crossed it <u>carelessly</u>. _____

5. On the other side, Penny smiled <u>darkly</u>. _____

6. We can rest and eat lunch <u>now</u>," she said. _____

B. Write an adverb from the word box to complete each sentence.

sleepily away back soon

1. Princess Penny yawned _____.

2. She leaned _____ and closed her eyes.

3. She _____ fell asleep and began to dream.

4. When Penny woke up, she saw that Copper had run _____.

C. Make up a short story about Penny or Copper. Write at least four sentences, and use adverbs to tell how, where, and when.

Copper's New Friend

A. Read the paragraph. Write an adverb from the word box to complete each sentence.

| loudly | finally | everywhere | slowly | happily |

"Copper, where are you?" Princess Penny screamed

_____. She searched _____ for him

but could not find him. So she walked _____ back to

the castle. When she _____ got there, Copper was

prancing _____ in the courtyard. A beautiful white

mare pranced with him.

B. Write each adverb under the correct heading.

| softly | tomorrow | often | there | quickly | ahead |

Tells How	Tells Where	Tells When
_____	_____	_____
_____	_____	_____

C. Pretend you live in a castle. Write a short story about something that happens there. Use at least two adverbs that tell how, one adverb that tells where, and one adverb that tells when.

A Chinese Festival

A. Circle the adverbs that compare two actions. Underline the adverbs that compare three or more actions. Make sure you include the word *more* or *most* when it is used to compare.

Tamra and her family went downtown to see the

Chinese New Year Festival. Her dad drove slower than usual.

There was so much city traffic. When they arrived, they had

to run more quickly than they expected. Tamra's brother

reached the stands and climbed higher than Mom and Dad

to find four seats. Tamra could see the most clearly because

she had binoculars. The drummers played the loudest of all

the groups. The festival was amazing!

B. Circle the correct adverb to complete each sentence.

1. The festival dragon moved (most gracefully, more gracefully) than a fire-breathing dragon.

2. When the dancing ended, Tamra raced (more quickly, most quickly) to the food court than her brother.

3. Tamra's brother gulped down his lunch (hungriest, most hungrily) of all, though!

C. Write a paragraph about a festival or fair you have attended. Use adverbs that compare in your paragraph.

St. Patrick's Day

A. Write words from the word box to complete the sentences.

slower longer most sooner earlier

I won't have to wait _____ than a

few days until St. Patrick's Day. The more excited I get,

the _____ the days move. Mom says that

the _____ I go to bed each night, the

_____ the day will come. I _____

often listen to my mom because she knows a thing or two!

B. Read the paragraph. Use the correct form of the adverb in parentheses to complete each sentence.

I don't think any family celebrates St. Patrick's Day

_____ (happily) than mine. My father steams

his corned beef _____ (long) than many recipes

say. He adds carrots, potatoes, and cabbage to the corned beef

_____ (late) than my mother does. We all fight to

see who can load their plates the _____ (high).

C. Write a paragraph about some fun family event. Use adverbs that compare in your paragraph.

Family Holidays

A. Proofread the paragraph. Cross out each incorrect adverb. Write the correct form of the adverb above it.

My family celebrates holidays oftener than anyone I know.

They have been doing this longest than I can remember. We have

the parties at our house because we can fit a big group the

more easily of all. My mother works more hard than usual to get

things ready. As it gets more closest to the time, people begin

arriving. Everyone brings something good to eat. It's so much fun!

B. Write *more* or *most* to complete each sentence correctly.

1. After dinner the cousins race to see who runs the _____ swiftly.

2. Cousin Tino runs _____ quickly than I do.

3. Tino runs _____ slowly than Cousin Gus, though.

4. Cousin Annie runs the _____ swiftly of us all.

5. Cousin Frankie glides the _____ gracefully. He likes to race on skates!

C. Write about a family holiday. Use five adverbs that compare in your descriptions.

We're Making a Collage!

A. Read the sentences. Circle the adjectives. Draw a line under the adverbs.

1. Mia and her friends wanted to make an interesting collage for school.

2. They quickly gathered a stack of magazines.

3. They cut colorful pictures to use in the collage.

4. They carefully glued the pictures on a piece of cardboard.

5. When they finally finished, they hung the picture in the hall at school.

B. Label the underlined word by writing *adjective* or *adverb* on the line.

1. The kids at school looked at the big collage   _____
   as they walked by it.

2. Students started putting comments on   _____
   colorful sticky notes next to the collage.

3. The number of comments quickly grew.   _____

4. Mia and her friends happily read the   _____
   comments.

5. They loved reading the nice things people   _____
   said about their work.

C. Write a paragraph about a project you have done with friends. Use adjectives and adverbs in your paragraph.

It's for the Birds!

A. Read the sentences. Add words from the chart to complete each sentence.

Adjectives	sloping	tall	tiny	wooden	one
Adverbs	quietly	carefully	suddenly	often	slowly

1. Pedro was building a birdhouse for the birds who
   _____ visited his backyard.

2. He glued together _____ sticks he had saved from
   ice-cream bars.

3. He _____ cut a hole for the birds to use to get into
   the birdhouse.

4. Pedro made a _____ roof and glued it on top.

5. He attached the birdhouse to a _____ stick and put
   it in the yard.

6. At first only _____ little bird visited the birdhouse.

7. Then another _____ bird joined the first one.

8. Pedro was surprised when _____ the yard was filled
   with birds.

9. His papi whispered _____, "Let's take a picture."

10. Papi _____ pushed the button and took the picture.

B. Write a paragraph about birds you have seen in your yard or in a park.
Use adjectives and adverbs to describe the birds.

Taking on a Project

A. Read the paragraph. Circle the incorrect adjective or adverb. Write the correct form above it.

      My friend Tomás and I were eagerly to make something fun for our art project. We soonly decided to make a mobile of the planets. Mobiles can be made of all kinds of greatly things. All you need is some string, a hanger, and some interestinger things to put together. We gathered markers, scissors, and some heavily cardboard. We quick cut out the planet shapes. Thenly we cut tiny holes at the top of the roundly shapes and threaded them with strings.

B. Write a paragraph about a project you and a classmate have made for school. Use four adjectives and three adverbs to describe what you made and how you made it.

Gators!

A. Write F (for _formal_) or I (for _informal_) above each underlined group of words.

Dear Jackson,

   Mom, Dad, and I had <u>quite an interesting time</u> at

Gatorland. It was <u>totally awesome</u>. There were <u>gators</u>

everywhere! We learned <u>many fascinating facts</u> about

alligators. These <u>guys</u> are really <u>cool</u>. <u>I hope to prepare a

report</u> on them for class.

<u>Sincerely yours</u>,

Kyle

B. Underline each sentence that is too informal for this report on alligators.

   Alligators almost became extinct. What bummer

news! American alligators were placed on the endangered

species list in 1967. By 1987 they were removed from the

endangered list. How great is that? There are now more

than a million American alligators. Pretty amazing, huh?

C. Write a short paragraph about an animal that interests you. Write it in formal language.

Visiting the Alligators in Florida

A. Circle *a.* or *b.* to show which sentence you would use for each type of writing.

1. Type of writing: a research report

   a. The alligator became the state reptile of Florida in 1987.

   b. If you wanna see gators, go to Florida.

2. Type of writing: a postcard to a friend

   a. Wow, these alligators are something to see!

   b. Alligators are considered a tourist attraction in Florida.

3. Type of writing: a letter to your teacher

   a. Man, you oughta see these guys!

   b. I think you would find the alligators very interesting.

B. Read the paragraph. Rewrite it to sound more formal.

My sis says gators are kinda creepy. I think they're totally cool. I'm gonna check them out on the Web.

_____

_____

_____

_____

_____

C. Imagine you are giving a report at school about a topic that interests you. Write the first paragraph.

Greetings

A. Read the informal sentences on the left. Draw a line from each one to the sentence that shows a more formal way of writing it.

1. No sweat.

2. Sorry.

3. That's gross!

4. Don't goof up.

5. You need to chill out.

a. Try to relax.

b. Try not to make a mistake.

c. That is really disgusting.

d. Please accept my apology.

e. That is not a problem.

B. Read the sentence pairs. Circle the informal sentence and underline the more formal one.

1. Boy, was it totally cool to visit Florida!

    It was a lot of fun to visit Florida!

2. We stayed in a nice hotel near the sights.

    Me and my parents had a cool room near most stuff.

3. The amusement parks were well worth the visit.

    Those parks were awesome!

4. My favorite activity was taking a cruise on the St. Johns River.

    Best thing, the St. Johns trip.

5. There were all kinds of gators and birds.

    We saw a lot of alligators and bald eagles.

C. Write a short letter to an older relative. Then rewrite it, changing a few words or phrases to make it an informal letter.

Mr. Larue's Cooking Class

A. Read the paragraph. Circle the adjectives that tell about the underlined nouns or pronouns.

Mr. Larue is a great <u>cook</u>. <u>He</u> is happy to share his skills with the children in the neighborhood. Every <u>Saturday</u> Mr. Larue has a class for ten <u>kids</u>. Today he is making a big <u>pot</u> of jambalaya. Mr. Larue shows the young <u>cooks</u> how to make it. The <u>children</u> are careful to do what he does. Mr. Larue uses a hot red <u>sauce</u>. His special <u>jambalaya</u> is spicy!

B. Read the paragraph. Circle the adverbs that tell about the underlined verbs.

Mr. Larue always <u>tells</u> stories while he cooks. We listen and <u>watch</u> him carefully. Then we slowly <u>follow</u> his directions. If we make a mistake, Mr. Larue kindly <u>corrects</u> us. He doesn't <u>treat</u> us harshly. That's why kids eagerly <u>join</u> Mr. Larue's cooking classes.

C. Write a paragraph about something you have learned in a class. Use adjectives and adverbs to describe it.

Learning More About Cooking

A. Circle the correct form of the adjective in parentheses. Then write the adjective on the line.

1. Carmine's chili is _____ than mine. (hotter, hot)

2. I sprinkle parsley on top of my chili, so it is _____

   than Carmine's. (more pretty, prettier)

3. The new student, Marita, is already the _____ cook

   of all. (successfullest, most successful)

4. Mr. Larue thinks Marita's chili is _____ than his.

   (tasty, tastier)

B. Read the paragraph. Cross out the mistakes with the adverbs that compare. Write the correct form above each crossed-out word.

   Mr. Larue prepares his dishes more careful than some of us.

He has cooked the longer of all. We're still learning. I'm trying to

mix the ingredients more slowlier so I won't forget something.

If I need to beat eggs, though, I have to stir them more quicker.

The electric mixer beats ingredients the most fastest.

C. Write a paragraph comparing two things you like to eat. Use adjectives and adverbs to compare them.

Open House at Mr. Larue's

A. Proofread the paragraph. Cross out each incorrect adjective or adverb and write the correct form above it. (Hint: There are 10 mistakes.)

We had a very successfully open house at Mr. Larue's last Saturday. Every one of the children in our cooking class made specially foods to serve. We made chili, submarine sandwiches, desserts—all kinds of yummiest foods. We spent many days careful preparing the food to get ready for Saturday. On the day of the open house, family members of all ages came to taste what we had happy cooked. Everyone total liked the food we made, and there were fewest leftovers when the open house was over. We were all so proudly! Nextest year we are going to train otherer young students to cook.

B. Write a paragraph about an open house you have been to at school or for an after-school class. Use formal language. Then change a few words or phrases to make it informal.

The Children's Book Store

A. Find each book title and cross it out. Write the title correctly above it.

There is a wonderful bookstore in our town called Books for Kids. They have every book you can imagine, from <u>little house on the prairie</u> to <u>dogzilla</u>. The other day I noticed a book that had just come in, <u>the case of the diamond dog collar</u>. I like mysteries, so I added it to my pile. I also picked up a copy of <u>encyclopedia brown and the case of the secret pitch</u>.

B. Write each book title correctly and underline it.

1. a wrinkle in time

   _____

2. mufaro's beautiful daughters

   _____

3. don't sit on my lunch

   _____

4. nate the great

   _____

5. jack and the wonder beans

   _____

C. Write a paragraph about two fiction books you like a lot. Make sure you underline the titles and capitalize them correctly.

Summer Knights

A. Read the paragraph. Find and underline three book titles. Write them correctly on the lines.

During the summer, Lincoln and his family like to go to the park to read. Last week Lincoln read danny, the champion of the world. His sister was reading the cricket in times square. This week Lincoln is going to read knights of the round table.

_____

_____

_____

B. Read the paragraph and find the book titles. Cross them out and rewrite them correctly above. Make sure to underline them.

Linc and Tran are writing a book about King Arthur. To research the topic, they read books on the subject, such as The sword in the stone, Legends Of king arthur, and The making of A Knight. They also read books about other characters from the King Arthur legends. Linc's favorite was Merlin And The Dragons. Tran's favorite was A pup in king Arthur's court.

C. Write a paragraph about two nonfiction books you have read and liked. Make sure you underline book titles and capitalize them correctly.

At the Book Fair

A. Proofread the passage. Cross out any words that have not been capitalized correctly in the book titles. Write them correctly above the crossed-out words.

Sam and his friend Chanase were excited about the book fair at their school. Sam found a copy of <u>duck on A Bike</u>, a picture book for his little sister. Chanase found <u>frindle</u>, a book about a boy who invents a new word for the pencil. Sam saw his favorite book, <u>diary of a wimpy Kid</u>. His best friend bought a copy. Sam decided to buy <u>Mummies In the morning</u>. Then Chanase found a mystery novel, <u>The secret of The Old mill</u>. The book fair raised lots of money for the school library.

B. Write a list of five books you would recommend to your friends. Make sure you underline the titles and capitalize them correctly.

Going to the Park

A. Read the paragraph and circle the contractions. Write the words that make up each contraction above the circled words.

There's a park in the neighborhood where Shantal lives. She loves to go there with her friends. The park used to be an ugly place. Children didn't feel safe there. People in the neighborhood have been cleaning it up. Once the park is all cleaned up, they'll post rules and enforce them. They've come up with a list of rules for people to follow: Don't litter. Put your trash in the trash bins. Don't hang out by yourself at the park. You're safer if you stick with a buddy.

B. Rewrite each sentence, using a contraction for the underlined words.

1. <u>We have</u> always wanted to make sure that students ride safely.

   _____

2. Tomorrow <u>I will</u> hand out the rules we want students to follow.

   _____

3. Ms. Sanchez has read the rules and thinks <u>they are</u> good.

   _____

C. Write a list of safety rules for a park. Make sure you write contractions correctly.

Cool at the Pool

A. Circle the words that can be replaced by contractions. Write the contractions above them.

      We are going to the community pool this Saturday. It is a

great pool, and my family loves going there. My big brother is the

lifeguard. He has been at the pool the last two summers. He is

a trained lifeguard, and he knows how to save people. We make

sure we do not break the rules when we are there. My brother

and my mom would never allow it.

B. Choose a contraction from the word box to complete each sentence correctly. Write them on the lines.

he's   haven't   we'll   she's   we're

1. I _____ missed a swimming class all summer.

2. My friend Mara has been sick, so _____ missed a few classes.

3. Six people are in my class, and _____ all good swimmers.

4. Next week _____ take part in a swim meet.

5. Mr. Kernan is making us practice a lot, and _____ a great coach.

C. Write a paragraph about a sport you play. Use contractions.

Don't Be a Fool on the Playground!

A. Proofread the passage. Cross out any contractions that have not been written correctly. Write them correctly above the crossed-out words.

Its important to behave on the school playground. Thats'

what our teacher, Ms. Shapiro, tells us, and shes right. If we dont

follow the playground rules, kids might get hurt. For example,

if you break a glass on the playground, itll shatter into sharp

pieces. A child might step on broken glass and get cut.

B. Read each sentence. Write the contraction above each set of underlined words.

1. I hope <u>we will</u> all learn to follow the rules on the playground.

2. Ms. Shapiro says <u>she will</u> make sure that students understand

    the rules.

3. Our class has promised that <u>we are</u> going to follow the rules.

4. <u>It is</u> great that we can work together!

5. We <u>do not</u> want our playground to become a dangerous place.

C. Write about some things you think people should not do on a playground. Use five contractions.

Wish You Were Here!

A. Read the postcard. Circle the comma in the body of the letter that separates a city name from a state name. Also circle the commas in the address.

Dear Papi,

    I hope you're well. I am having a good time with Mami visiting our cousins in Franklin, Massachusetts. I'm learning about being a ranger. I can't wait to tell you all about it.

Love,

Roberto

Mr. Mateo Gonzales

112 Jupiter Way, Apartment 27

Houston, TX 77006

B. Read the addresses. Circle each comma that separates the street name from the apartment number. Draw a box around each comma that separates the city name from the state name.

Gus Medina

77 107th Street, Apartment 3

Detroit, MI 48207

Jason Lin

2371 San Pablo Street, #117

Phoenix, AZ 85085

C. Write a letter to someone in your family about a place you have visited. Write the address on an envelope.

From Me to You

A. Read the addresses for the letter. Add commas where they belong.

535 Jackson Drive Suite 222

Atlanta GA 30306

Mr. Jonti Singh

8 Sullivan Way #2

Bridgewater NJ 08807

October 12, 2017

Dear Jonti,

I was so glad to get your letter. We can't wait to see you next week. We have all kinds of fun things planned. See you soon!

Love,

Uncle Hari

B. Read the addresses on the envelope. Add commas where they belong.

Erica Jacoby

747 Concord Lane Unit 43

Sacramento CA 95825

Santana Washington

1812 Campos Street Apartment 4

Los Angeles CA 90021

C. Write a letter to a friend who lives in another town. Use commas correctly in your address and your friend's address.

Dear Aunt Julia

A. Find four mistakes with commas in the addresses. Circle each comma that is in the wrong place. Draw an arrow from it to where it belongs.

Martin Watkins

3 Summer, Street Apt. 2

Hampton NH, 03842

Mrs. Julia Zahn

428, Jackson Avenue Unit 47

St., Martin MS 39532

B. Add the missing commas where they belong.

Helen Grush

3 Summer Street Apt. 2

Hampton NH 03842

Ms. Patti Bloston

24520 Shady Brook Lane

Carmel CA 93923

C. Write a letter to a family member about something you would like to do when you grow up. Write your address at the top of the letter. Write your family member's address on an envelope. Make sure you use commas correctly.

The Big Apple

A. Circle the quotation marks. Underline each comma that separates a speaker's words from the speaker.

"I just found out that New York is called the Big Apple," Toni told her grandmother.

"I didn't know that," Mrs. Crowe replied to her granddaughter.

"Maybe everyone in New York really likes apples," said Toni.

Her grandmother smiled and replied, "Maybe it rains apple juice there."

"Maybe all the houses are made from apples," laughed Toni.

Her grandmother looked at her and said, "Maybe we should go to New York to see for ourselves."

"Let's go," said Toni.

B. Write a dialogue between two people who are talking about a fascinating fact. Use quotation marks and commas correctly.

Jack and the Daisy

A. Read the story. Add any missing quotation marks and commas.

"Jack, please don't pick me" said the daisy.

"I didn't know daisies could talk, Jack replied.

Well, this daisy can, so please don't pick me, said the daisy.

"I'm sorry, but I have to pick you" Jack answered. My sister

isn't well, and I thought a daisy might cheer her up."

"I have an idea" said the daisy.

"Tell me Jack replied.

Plant me in a flowerpot, and I'll live in your sister's room

forever" the daisy explained.

"My sister would love that" Jack replied. "I think that's

a great idea

B. Write a dialogue between Jack's sister and the daisy. Use quotation marks to show each speaker's exact words. Add commas to set off the speakers' words from the person speaking.

Going to a Concert

A. Proofread the dialogue. Add any missing quotation marks and commas.

"Dad, I'd like to go see the Jensen Boys concert on Friday night, Bella said to her father.

"No" he replied. "I don't want you at a concert alone.

"I wouldn't be going alone, Bella replied. "Shayna, Ali, and Emma are going, too."

Bella's father replied "You need an adult to go with you.

What a great idea, Dad," Bella said as she hugged her father. "You can come with us. Then all the parents will be happy.

Hmmm," Bella's father said as he rubbed his chin. "Aren't you the clever one!

B. Imagine what the concert was like with Bella, her friends, and her father. Write at least five more lines of dialogue between Bella and her father about the concert. Use commas and quotation marks correctly.

We're Reading All the Time!

A. Rewrite each book title on the line. Capitalize the words in each title. correctly. Then draw a line under the title.

1. the cat in the hat

   _____

2. anansi the spider

   _____

3. chang and the bamboo flute

   _____

4. the boy of a thousand faces

   _____

B. Read the contractions. Write the words that make up each contraction.

1. isn't _____

2. we'll _____

3. I've _____

4. you're _____

C. Write a paragraph recommending a book that you've read. Use at least two contractions.

Don't Forget to Write!

A. Read the addresses. Add commas where they belong.

Matt Bellamy

17 Lions Lane #2

Carson City NV 89701

Andy Shanahan

2731 Cobalt Street Apartment 7

Wilkes-Barre PA 18711

B. Read the letter. Cross out any words that could be replaced by a contraction. Write the contraction above the crossed-out words.

Dear Mags,

I heard you are having fun on vacation. We will be

leaving on our trip soon. I think it is going to be fun

visiting my cousins. I have never been to St. Louis before.

I am sure you will hear all about it when we get back. See

you in a month!

Your friend,

Tamara

C. Write a letter to a friend. Write your address at the top of the letter. Write your friend's address on an envelope. Make sure you use commas correctly.

What Are You Doing Here?

A. Proofread this dialogue between Antoine and Jake. Add missing quotation marks and commas where they belong.

Antoine ran into his friend Jake at the grocery store.

"Hey, Jake! What are you doing here? Antoine asked.

Jake smiled and said My dad wanted to pick up

something special."

Antoine looked around. Then he said, "Oh, I see your

dad over there.

Jake replied He had to have this special sauce for a

dish he's making."

I wish my dad cooked" Antoine said, laughing.

Jake laughed and said, "You sound like my mom!

Antoine turned and said, Enjoy your dinner!

Jake waved and said "See you on Monday, Antoine.

B. Write a dialogue between two friends who run into each other. Use commas and quotation marks correctly.

Student Grammar Guide

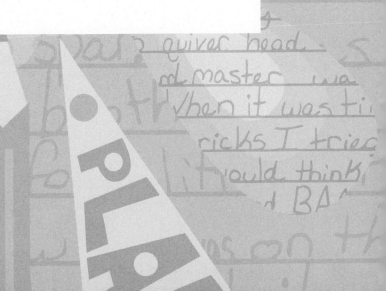

Sentences

A **sentence** is a group of words that expresses a complete thought. It includes a subject and a predicate.

- The **subject** tells whom or what the sentence is about.

  <u>My whole family</u> goes to the carnival every year.

- The **predicate** tells what the subject does or is.

  We <u>go on the Ferris wheel</u>. It <u>is our favorite ride</u>.

An **incomplete sentence** does not express a complete thought. It is missing either a subject or a predicate.

Incomplete sentence: Wins a prize at the game booth.

Complete sentence: <u>My big brother</u> wins a prize at the game booth.

Incomplete sentence: My little sister.

Complete sentence: My little sister <u>picks a stuffed tiger for a prize</u>.

A **compound sentence** is made up of two simple sentences joined by the **conjunctions**, or connecting words, *and*, *but*, or *or*. Put a comma before the conjunction.

I have gone to the Fun House**,** <u>and</u> I am now on the Teacups.

I can stop for a snack now**,** <u>or</u> I can go to a game booth.

I want to ride on the Whirl-and-Twirl**,** <u>but</u> I am too small.

A **complex sentence** is made up of one group of words that tells a complete thought and one group of words that does not. Complex sentences use conjunctions like *after*, *before*, *because*, and *until*. No comma is needed before the conjunction.

I have to wait <u>until</u> I am two inches taller.

My brother doesn't like that ride <u>because</u> it makes him dizzy.

Becca didn't eat anything <u>before</u> she went on the Whirl-and-Twirl.

She had a great big smile on her face <u>when</u> the ride was over.

Nouns

A **noun** is a word that names a person, a place, a thing, an animal, or an idea. A noun can be singular or plural. A **singular noun** names one. A **plural noun** names more than one.

- Add *-s* to form the plural of most nouns: bee<u>s</u>, flower<u>s</u>.

- Add *-es* to nouns that end with *s*, *x*, *sh*, *ch*: bus<u>es</u>, box<u>es</u>, lunch<u>es</u>, wish<u>es</u>.

- Change the *y* to an *i* and add *-es* to a noun that ends with a consonant + *y*: story − *y* + *i* + *es* = stor<u>ies</u>; family − *y* + *i* + *es* = famil<u>ies</u>.

- Change the spelling to form the plural of some irregular nouns: mouse/m<u>ice</u>; goose/g<u>ee</u>se; child/child<u>ren</u>.

A **<u>common noun</u>** names any person, place, or thing. It does not begin with a capital letter. A **<u>proper noun</u>** names a specific person, place, or thing. It begins with a capital letter.

My favorite <u>city</u> is <u>New York City</u>.

<u>Broadway</u> is the longest <u>street</u> in the <u>city</u>.

You can climb to the <u>top</u> of a famous <u>statue</u> called the <u>Statue of Liberty</u>.

A **possessive noun** shows ownership.

- Add *'s* to make singular nouns possessive: the robin**'**<u>s</u> egg.

- Add an apostrophe after the *s* for plurals that end with *s*: the robin<u>s</u>**'** nest.

- Add *'s* to an irregular plural noun that does not end with *s*: the children**'**<u>s</u> playground.

Pronouns

A **subject pronoun** replaces a noun that is the subject of a sentence.
It tells whom or what the sentence is about.

Bees fly from flower to flower.

They fly from flower to flower.

An **object pronoun** replaces a noun that receives the action of the verb.
It can also follow a word such as *for*, *from*, *to*, or *with*.

Bees gather pollen from flowers.   Bees also carry pollen to flowers.
Bees gather it from flowers.   Bees also carry pollen to them.

A **possessive pronoun** takes the place of a noun and shows ownership.

A flower uses the pollen to make its seeds.

My parents love gardening. That is their favorite hobby.
Drawing flowers is mine.

A pronoun must **agree in number** with the noun it is replacing. Singular
pronouns replace singular nouns. Plural pronouns replace plural nouns.

Rob and Alexa were playing catch.   Rob heard a bee buzzing.
They were playing catch.   He heard a bee buzzing.

A pronoun must also **agree in gender** with the noun it is replacing.
She and *her* replace one female. *He* and *his* replace one male.

Alexa tried to swat the bee away.   The bee stung Alexa.
She tried to swat the bee away.   The bee stung her.

Rob went to get the first aid kit.
He went to get the first aid kit.

Verbs

A **verb** tells what someone or something does or is like.

An **action verb** tells what someone or something does.

Gabriella <u>hits</u> the baseball. Her teammates <u>cheer</u>.

- An action verb can have two parts—a **main verb** and a **helping verb**. The helping verb usually comes before the main verb and does not show action.

Gabriella <u>can</u> <u>run</u> fast. She <u>has</u> <u>reached</u> third base.

A **linking verb** connects the subject to words that tell what the subject is or is like.

Gabriella <u>is</u> a good player. She <u>feels</u> proud.

- Linking verbs can also have <u>main verbs</u> and <u>helping verbs</u>.

The game <u>will</u> <u>be</u> over soon. It <u>has</u> <u>been</u> a fun game.

A verb **tense** tells when the action in a sentence takes place.

- A **present-tense** verb tells about something happening now.

Louis <u>catches</u> the ball. His friends <u>yell</u>, "Hooray!"

- A **past-tense** verb tells about something that has already happened. Some past-tense verbs are formed with *-ed*, but others are irregular.

The game <u>ended</u>. People in the stands <u>clapped</u>.

The players <u>shook</u> hands. They <u>ran</u> off the field.

- A **future-tense** verb tells about something that is going to happen. It includes the helping verb *will*.

The two teams <u>will play</u> again next week.

A verb must **agree in number** with its subject.

- When the subject is singular, use the singular form of the verb or helping verb.

  This cap <u>belongs</u> to Ramona. She <u>is</u> standing over there.

- When the subject is plural, use the plural form of the verb or helping verb.

  Those boys always <u>bring</u> the bats for the game.

  They <u>are</u> collecting the bats now.

Adjectives

An **adjective** is a word that describes, or tells more about, a noun or a pronoun.

- Adjectives can describe many things, such as *size*, *shape*, and *color*. They can also describe how something *looks*, *sounds*, *smells*, *tastes*, or *feels*.

  The storm made a size shape <u>big</u> <u>round</u> puddle in the yard.

  Splash! Now my color <u>white</u> dog is color <u>brown</u>.

- An adjective can also tell *how many* or *how much*.

  how many My <u>two</u> friends helped me wash my dog.

  how much We had <u>a little</u> help from my brothers.

Adjectives have special forms that can be used to show how two or more people, places, animals, or things are different.

- Use *-er* to compare two people, places, animals, or things.

  The sun is <u>hotter</u> today than it was yesterday.

- Use *-est* to compare three or more people, places, animals, or things.

  That was the <u>prettiest</u> sunset I have ever seen.

- Not all adjectives use *-er* or *-est* to compare things. Some use different words.

  Jocelyn's scary story was really <u>bad</u>!

  Jacob's scary story was even <u>worse</u> than Jocelyn's.

  Mackenzie's scary story was the <u>worst</u> of all.

Adverbs

Adverbs are words that tell more about a verb. They tell *how*, *when*, or *where* something happens. Most adverbs that tell how end with *-ly*.

- How: *quickly, loudly, sadly, softly, nicely*

  The wind whispers <u>softly</u> through the leaves.

- Where: *outside, here, there, away, down*

  I like to sit <u>outside</u> in the shade of a tree.

- When: *today, tomorrow, suddenly, later, next, now*

  I will read <u>now</u> and play with my friends <u>later</u>.

Adverbs have special forms that can be used to <u>compare actions</u>.

- Use *-er* to compare two actions.

  A hare moves <u>faster</u> than a tortoise.

- Use *-est* to compare three or more actions.

  A cheetah runs the <u>fastest</u> of any animal on Earth.

- When an adverb is a long word, use *more* or *most* instead of *-er* or *-est* to compare.

  Jeb works <u>carefully</u> on his math homework.

  He works <u>more carefully</u> on division than on multiplication.

  He works <u>most carefully</u> of all on his word problems.

Capitalization and Punctuation

The first and last words in a book title, and all the important words in between, are capitalized.

This week we're reading the book *The Mouse and the Motorcycle*.

Our group also liked the book *A Letter to Amy*.

Next week we're going to read the book *Casey at the Bat*.

My favorite book so far is *Bartholomew and the Oobleck*.

My friend Jesse's favorite book is *Mirette on the High Wire*.

I'm writing a book report on *Encyclopedia Brown Saves the Day*.

A **contraction** is two words joined together to make a shorter word. An apostrophe (') takes the place of the letter or letters that have been left out.

is + not = isn't	he + is = he's	I + will = I'll
was + not = wasn't	she + has = she's	you + have = you've
are + not = aren't	it + is = it's	they + are = they're

Commas are used to set off information in the parts of a letter. Use commas to separate a street name from an apartment, a city name from a state name, and the day from the year. Also use a comma after the greeting in the letter and to separate the closing from the signature.

153 Oval Street, Unit 4

Gary, IN 46408

April 24, 2014

Use a comma after the greeting in the letter.

Dear Anika,

Gosh, it's good to hear from you! I'm glad you like your new home in Portland, Maine. It'll be good to see you next summer. Summer isn't that far away.

Use a comma to separate a city name from a state name in a sentence.

Your friend,

Tyler

Use a comma to separate the closing from the signature.

(continues)

Capitalization and Punctuation *(continued)*

Quotation marks are used to set off the exact words of a speaker, and a comma often separates the speaker's exact words from the rest of the sentence. Ending punctuation always goes inside the quotation marks.

Sophie said, "I think Book Club is really fun."

> Use quotation marks to let readers know which words speakers are saying.

Her friend Trey said, "I do too, but I don't say much."

> Use a comma to separate what the speaker is saying from the rest of the sentence.

"Why don't you speak more?" Sophie asked.

Trey replied, "I'm afraid I'll give the wrong answer."

> Always put end punctuation inside the quotation marks.

Tasks

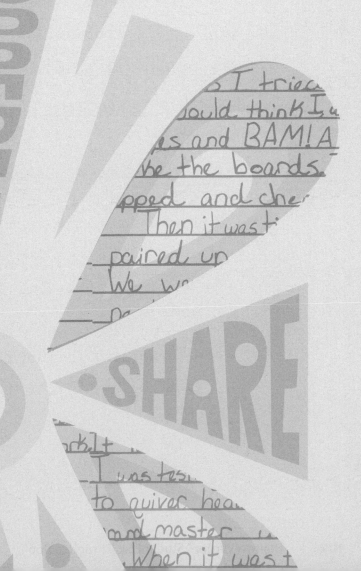

Task 1

A student is writing a story. Draw a line under the correct answers to finish the sentences.

(1) I found something interesting _____ I went to Grandma's house. (2) In one of the closets, I saw a box of old books for _____. (3) I _____ up the box and took it to the kitchen. (4) Grandma was there, packing our lunch.

(5) "Grandma, are these your books? I asked.

(6) "No" she answered. (7) "Those were your _____ books." (8) The one on top was titled *How to train a Puppy*. (9) I _____ the book. (10) I saw a _____ handwriting. (11) It said, "This book belongs to Ruth Ann Martin, who lives at 10 Garden Street Tampa, Florida." (12) My mom wrote this when _____ was a little girl!

1. Which word correctly completes sentence 1?
   a. when
   b. since
   c. until

2. Which word correctly completes sentence 2?
   a. children
   b. childs
   c. child

3. Which one correctly completes sentence 3?

    a. pick

    b. picked

    c. will pick

4. Which is the correct way to write sentence 5?

    a. "Grandma, are these your books?" I asked.

    b. "Grandma, are these your books? I asked."

    c. Correct as is

5. Which is the correct way to write sentence 6?

    a. "No, she answered."

    b. "No," she answered.

    c. Correct as is

6. Which word correctly completes sentence 7?

    a. mothers

    b. mothers'

    c. mother's

7. Which is the correct way to write the title in sentence 8?

    a. *How to train a puppy*

    b. *How to Train a Puppy*

    c. Correct as is

8. Which one correctly completes sentence 9?

    a. open

    b. will open

    c. opened

9. Which word correctly completes sentence 10?

    a. child

    b. child's

    c. childs'

GO ON

10. Which is the correct way to write the underlined part of sentence 11?

   a. 10 Garden Street, Tampa, Florida.

   b. 10 Garden Street, Tampa Florida.

   c. Correct as is

11. Which word correctly completes sentence 12?

   a. they

   b. her

   c. she

Here is more of the story. Draw a line under the correct answers to finish the sentences.

(13) I _____ home from Grandma's house with a big box of books. (14) Mom was really surprised, _____ she started digging in the box. (15) "Here it is!" she exclaimed. "I've found *The Wind in the willows*. (16) This was the book I liked _____ of all. (17) Your Uncle Mike loved this book, too."

(18) My Uncle Mike _____ near us now. (19) He used to live in <u>Denver Colorado</u>. (20) He moved here two _____ ago for a new job. (21) Yesterday I _____ excited to see Uncle Mike in our house. (22) He was even _____ than my mom when I gave him the book.

12. Which word correctly completes sentence 13?

   a. goed

   b. went

   c. wented

13. Which word correctly completes sentence 14?

   a. but

   b. and

   c. or

14. Which is the correct way to write the title in sentence 15?

   a. *The Wind in the Willows*

   b. *The wind in The Willows*

   c. Correct as is

15. Which word correctly completes sentence 16?

   a. better

   b. bestest

   c. best

16. Which word correctly completes sentence 18?

   a. live

   b. lives

   c. lived

17. Which is the correct way to write the underlined part of sentence 19?

   a. Denver, Colorado

   b. Denver Colorado,

   c. Correct as is

18. Which word correctly completes sentence 20?

   a. month

   b. months

   c. monthes

GO ON

19. Which word correctly completes sentence 21?

    a. feel

    b. feeled

    c. felt

20. Which word correctly completes sentence 22?

    a. happyer

    b. happier

    c. happiest

Name: _____ Date: _____

Task 2

A student is writing a story. Draw a line under the correct answers to finish the sentences.

---

(1) Kai is flying to California next week to see his _____,
Dave and Dan. (2) It is Dave's birthday, _____ Kai will join
the boys and their parents for vacation. (3) They _____ at a
campground near the beach. (4) Kai always has a good time with
his _____ family.

(5) "Dave sent me his address, so we can mail his present,"
Kai told his mom. (6) "He _____ to my e-mail just a few
minutes ago."

(7) "I'll also send those shoes Dave left here last summer.
Mom said. (8) "Dave's feet are probably _____ than they were
last year, but the shoes may fit Dan."

---

1. Which word correctly completes sentence 1?

   a. cousins

   b. cousin

   c. cousin's

2. Which word correctly completes sentence 2?

   a. but

   b. and

   c. since

GO ON

3. Which one correctly completes sentence 3?

    a. stay

    b. stayed

    c. will stay

4. Which word correctly completes sentence 4?

    a. cousins

    b. cousins'

    c. cousin's

5. Which is the correct way to write sentence 5?

    a. "Dave sent me his address, so we can mail his present." Kai told his mom.

    b. "Dave sent me his address, so we can mail his present, Kai told his mom."

    c. Correct as is

6. Which word correctly completes sentence 6?

    a. reply

    b. replyed

    c. replied

7. Which is the correct way to write sentence 7?

    a. "I'll also send those shoes Dave left here last summer," Mom said.

    b. "I'll also send those shoes Dave left here last summer, Mom said."

    c. Correct as is

8. Which word correctly completes sentence 8?

    a. big

    b. bigger

    c. biggest

Read this e-mail. Draw a line under the correct answers.

From: Dave

To: Kai

Subject: Summer fun!

(9) This is going to be the _____ summer ever! (10) The campgrounds are at <u>1404 Bayside, Street</u>. (11) They have a great beach, and they also have a few _____. (12) Last July I _____ on the beach every morning. (13) You can use _____ swim fins. (14) Dan has grown so much that they don't fit _____ anymore.

(15) I just finished a book titled the *Best science fiction Stories of All Time*. (16) This book _____ my favorite now. (17) Last year you _____ the story "the thing from Venus." (18) One story in the book is like that one, _____ the ending is different.

(19) I know that your mom asked for my mailing address. (20) It is <u>643 Luna Street Pasadena, CA 91107</u>.

---

9. Which one correctly completes sentence 9?
   a. more exciting
   b. excitingest
   c. most exciting

10. Which is the best way to write the underlined part of sentence 10?
    a. 1404 Bayside Street
    b. 1404, Bayside Street
    c. Correct as is

GO ON

11. Which word correctly completes sentence 11?

   a. pony

   b. ponies

   c. ponys

12. Which word correctly completes sentence 12?

   a. run

   b. runned

   c. ran

13. Which is the correct way to complete sentence 13?

   a. Dans'

   b. Dan's

   c. Dans's

14. Which word correctly completes sentence 14?

   a. her

   b. him

   c. them

15. Which is the correct way to write the title in sentence 15?

   a. *The Best Science Fiction Stories of All Time*

   b. *The best Science Fiction Stories Of All Time*

   c. Correct as is

16. Which word correctly completes sentence 16?

   a. is

   b. are

   c. was

17. Which one correctly completes sentence 17?

   a. enjoy

   b. enjoyed

   c. will enjoy

18. Which is the correct way to write the title in sentence 17?

    a. "The Thing from Venus"

    b. "The thing From Venus"

    c. Correct as is

19. Which word correctly completes sentence 18?

    a. and

    b. or

    c. but

20. Which is the correct way to write the underlined part of sentence 20?

    a. 643 Luna Street Pasadena CA 91107

    b. 643 Luna Street, Pasadena, CA 91107

    c. Correct as is

STOP

Task 3

A student wrote a letter to a friend. Draw a line under the correct answers to finish the sentences.

(1) 75 Teaberry, Lane

(2) Cleveland Ohio 44130

(3) June 20, 2019

(4) Dear Milo,

    (5) Mom says your family is coming here for the Fourth of July. **(6)** When I heard that, I _____ a cartwheel! **(7)** We'll go to the parade in the morning, _____ we'll have a picnic afterward. **(8)** I am already dreaming of _____ apple pie. **(9)** After the picnic we'll swim in the pool. **(10)** Last year I _____ in the water with my clothes on! **(11)** This year we'll put on our suits and wear fins on our _____. **(12)** The fireworks will start _____ it gets dark. **(13)** They will probably be even _____ than last year. **(14)** We can watch them from the _____.

1. Which is the correct way to write line 1?
    a. 75 Teaberry Lane
    b. 75, Teaberry Lane
    c. Correct as is

2. Which is the correct way to write line 2?

   a. Cleveland Ohio, 44130

   b. Cleveland, Ohio 44130

   c. Correct as is

3. Which word correctly completes sentence 6?

   a. do

   b. doed

   c. did

4. Which word correctly completes sentence 7?

   a. but

   b. or

   c. and

5. Which one correctly completes sentence 8?

   a. Aunt Ritas

   b. Aunt Rita's

   c. Aunt Ritas'

6. Which word correctly completes sentence 10?

   a. fall

   b. falled

   c. fell

7. Which word correctly completes sentence 11?

   a. foot

   b. foots

   c. feet

8. Which word correctly completes sentence 12?

   a. when

   b. until

   c. so

GO ON

9. Which word correctly completes sentence 13?

   a. big

   b. bigger

   c. biggest

10. Which word correctly completes sentence 14?

   a. benchs

   b. benchis

   c. benches

Here is the rest of the letter. Correct all the errors you find.

(15) I have other great news! (16) I will be marching with the school band in the parade. (17) I have been learning to play "the Stars And Stripes Forever." (18) I use my older _____ trumpet. (19) Next month I _____ on my very own trumpet. (20) Luckily, I don't have to play "the Star-Spangled Banner." (21) It's the _____ song ever written! (22) Last week I tried to play it. (23) My brother yelled, "Vicky, stop that awful noise!"

(24) Then Mom _____, "Leave your sister alone. (25) _____ needs to practice."

(26) "There aren't enough years in a lifetime for her to learn that song" my brother shouted back. (27) Even I had to laugh. (28) I _____ to play a different song for you next week!

Your cousin,

Vicky

11. Which is the correct way to write the title in sentence 17?

    a. "The Stars and Stripes Forever"

    b. "The Stars and stripes forever"

    c. Correct as is

12. Which word goes in the blank in sentence 18?

    a. brother

    b. brothers'

    c. brother's

13. Which one correctly completes sentence 19?

    a. play

    b. played

    c. will play

14. Which is the correct way to write the title in sentence 20?

    a. "the star-spangled banner"

    b. "The Star-Spangled Banner"

    c. Correct as is

15. Which one correctly completes sentence 21?

    a. difficulter

    b. difficultest

    c. most difficult

16. Which is the correct way to write sentence 23?

    a. My brother yelled, Vicky, stop that awful noise.

    b. My brother yelled "Vicky, stop that awful noise."

    c. Correct as is

17. Which one correctly completes sentence 24?

    a. hollers

    b. hollered

    c. will holler

18. Which word correctly completes sentence 25?

  a. It

  b. He

  c. She

19. Which is the correct way to write sentence 26?

  a. "There aren't enough years in a lifetime for her to learn that song," my brother shouted back.

  b. "There aren't enough years in a lifetime for her to learn that song, my brother shouted back."

  c. Correct as is

20. Which word correctly completes sentence 28?

  a. promise

  b. promises

  c. promising